She wanted to know her child...
She was flooded by an irresistible peace,
She understood she was holding something
She loved so much,
She did not know what else to do...

Guy de Maupassant

For Pierre

Concept: Diane Barbara
The authors would like to thank the following people for their help:
The documentation service of the Parents' School and all the children
who did such a good job of "putting on their thinking caps" about the topic of their mothers,
in particular the students of CM2 (2001) of Stanislas College.

Diane Barbara and Christine Donnier

Mom and Me

Harry N. Abrams, Inc., Publishers

No matter where you are in the world, you are sure to find a lot of moms: small ones, tall ones, young ones, older ones! There will be athletic moms, moms who love books, overwhelmed moms, and very organized ones, too. You will find rushed moms and more relaxed ones, moms in blue jeans and moms in suits, the kinds of moms who love to cuddle and snuggle and the kinds of moms who are stricter, too… There are all sorts of very wonderful and special moms.

Moms…moms…
Imagine a river of them. Though each one is unique,
they share the great fortune of having children they love very much!

This album is for memories, both old ones and new ones.
It is to be filled in by you and your mom together so that you will learn
more about each other than you already know and grow to love each
other more than you already do!

Like a House...

Some say that a mom is like a house, for she protects her child like a shelter from the rain and winds of life. Others think that a mom is like the sun. For she knows how to keep her child warm when life becomes cold and gray. There are those who believe that a mom is soft and sweet, like the fruit of a tree that nurtures. And there are still others who think that a mom is all of these things and much more... These people say, "A mom? Why, she is life itself!"

Life Before You Were Born

Moms are very lucky, for they are often the first ones to feel that you are here. They come to know you as you grow and move inside of them. And today, through ultrasound, your mom and your dad can also get to see you before you are born!

Ultrasound of myself at ———— weeks

Glue your ultrasound photo above.
Where is your head? Where are your feet?
Mom, please explain everything—with the help of arrows, of course!

Tell me, Mom...

Mom, please tell me about my life inside of you!

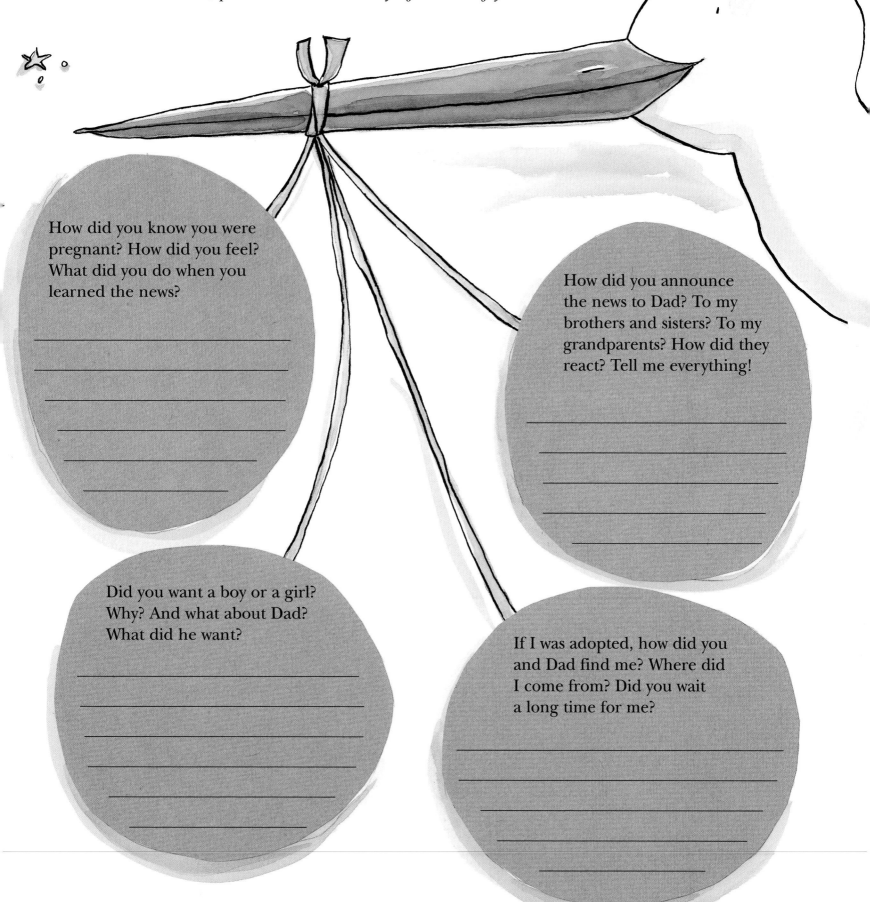

How did you know you were pregnant? How did you feel? What did you do when you learned the news?

_____

_____

_____

_____

How did you announce the news to Dad? To my brothers and sisters? To my grandparents? How did they react? Tell me everything!

_____

_____

_____

_____

Did you want a boy or a girl? Why? And what about Dad? What did he want?

_____

_____

_____

_____

If I was adopted, how did you and Dad find me? Where did I come from? Did you wait a long time for me?

_____

_____

_____

_____

How did you and Dad
prepare for my arrival?

_____

_____

_____

_____

_____

_____

FOR TWINS OR MORE!
And if there were more than
one of us, what did you
and Dad think?

_____

_____

_____

_____

_____

Photo of Mom pregnant or
a photo of when I was adopted

Date: **Place:**

8

My Birth

To have or adopt a child is like plunging into mysterious water— the water of an upcoming life that is filled with love. And even if a mom has had other babies, for her, each new birth is another journey.

Tell me, Mom, who cut my umbilical cord?
_____
_____

Date of my birth:_____

Where and at what time was I born?_____

What was the weather like that day? _____

Which day of the week was it? _____

How did it go? _____
_____
_____

What did I look like when you first saw me? _____
_____
_____

What did you think? What did you say?_____
_____

Did you take me in your arms right away? If yes, how did you feel?_____
_____
_____

Was Dad there? If yes, what did he say or do?_____
_____
_____

Were there other people there, too?_____

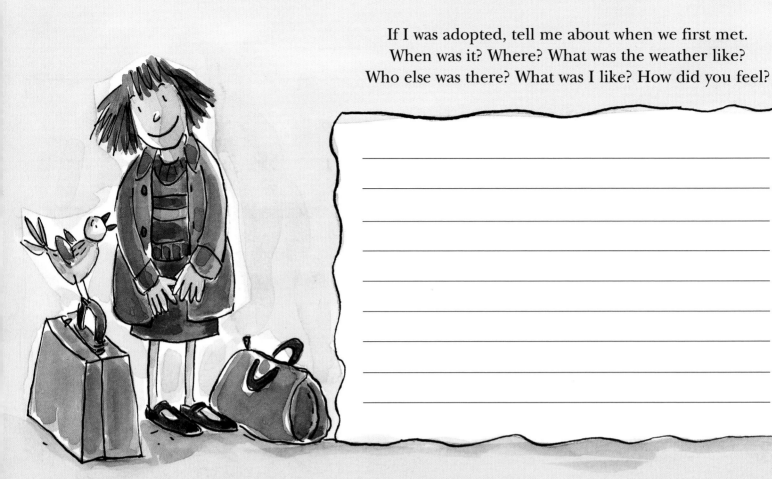

If I was adopted, tell me about when we first met.
When was it? Where? What was the weather like?
Who else was there? What was I like? How did you feel?

_____

_____

_____

_____

_____

_____

_____

_____

A few more questions about my arrival!

How did you choose my name?_____
_____

If I had been of the opposite sex, what would you have called me?_____
_____

Whom did you and Dad first tell about my birth? _____
_____

Where and when did my brothers and sisters see me for the first time? _____
_____

How did they react? _____
_____
_____

Who else besides my sisters and brothers came to see me right away? _____
_____
_____

First photo of me with Mom

Tell me, Mom, how much older are you than me?
_____
_____

At _____ **hours!**   **Place:** _____

What were our first days at home together like?

How did we get home and what was the weather like that day? _____
_____

Where did we live and where did I sleep? _____
_____

How did you feed me and who else took care of me? _____
_____

What was my first toy? _____
_____

What kind of new baby was I? Was I quiet? Did I cry a lot? Was I always hungry? _____

What did you like best to do with me? _____
_____

Did you sing me lullabies or songs? If yes, which ones? Write me a few lines from them… _____
_____
_____

11

My Firsts

Since your mom has known you longer than anyone else, ask her to tell you about the "first times" of your life...

Here are ideas of "first times" to write or draw in. Give as many details as possible, of course!

My first word ...
(Where? What age?)

_____

_____

_____

My first steps...
(Where? What age?)

_____

_____

_____

My first toy or
stuffed animal...
(Its name? What did it
look like?)

_____

_____

_____

The first naughty thing I did...

_____

_____

_____

My first vacation…
(Where did we go? What did we do?)

My first day at day care, the nursery, or with my nanny…

My first friend…
(What was his or her name? Where did we meet? What did he or she look like?)

My first birthday
(How did we celebrate? Who was there?)

Tell me, Mom, do you remember the first time I said "Mama"?

13

My Life As a Toddler

When you were very little, you needed your mom very, very often, like a baby bird needs its mother's wing. There, close to her, you grew into a toddler and became stronger!

Glue a photo of yourself, between the ages of 2 and 4 years old, in the middle of this page. Then ask your mom to answer these questions about when you were a toddler:

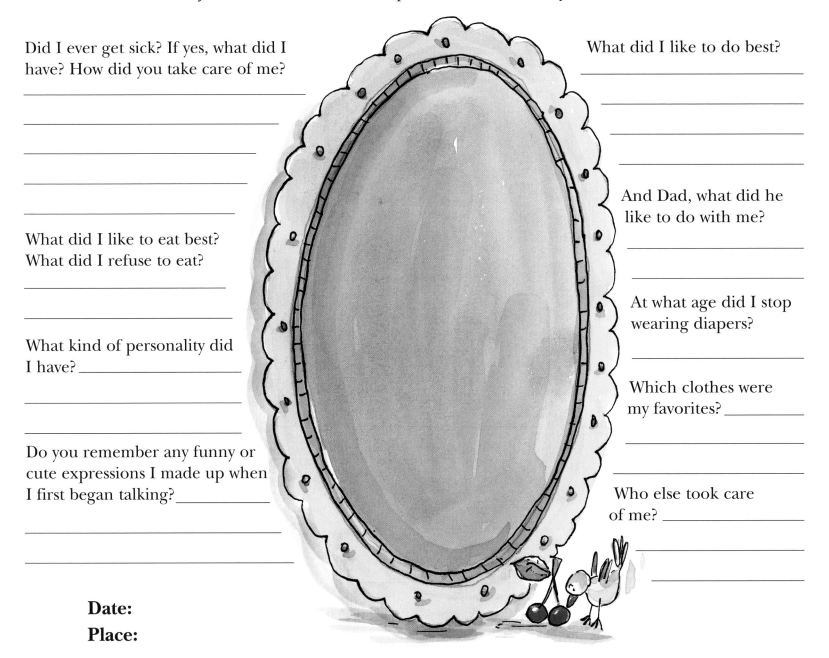

Did I ever get sick? If yes, what did I have? How did you take care of me?

_____

_____

_____

_____

What did I like to eat best? What did I refuse to eat?

_____

_____

What kind of personality did I have? _____

_____

_____

Do you remember any funny or cute expressions I made up when I first began talking? _____

_____

_____

What did I like to do best?

_____

_____

_____

And Dad, what did he like to do with me?

_____

_____

At what age did I stop wearing diapers?

_____

Which clothes were my favorites? _____

_____

_____

Who else took care of me? _____

_____

Date:

Place:

✎ My First Day of School

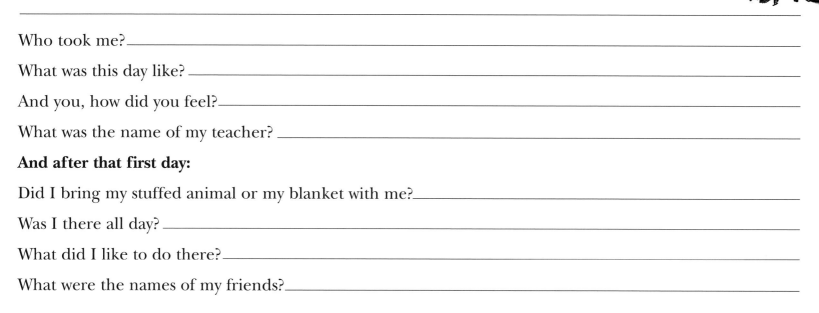

On your first day of school, everything was topsy-turvy!
And although you might not have thought so,
it was also a big day in your mom's life.

Tell me, Mom...

When was my first day of school? Where was my school? How old was I when I started?

_____

Who took me?_____

What was this day like? _____

And you, how did you feel?_____

What was the name of my teacher? _____

And after that first day:

Did I bring my stuffed animal or my blanket with me?_____

Was I there all day? _____

What did I like to do there?_____

What were the names of my friends?_____

My first school picture

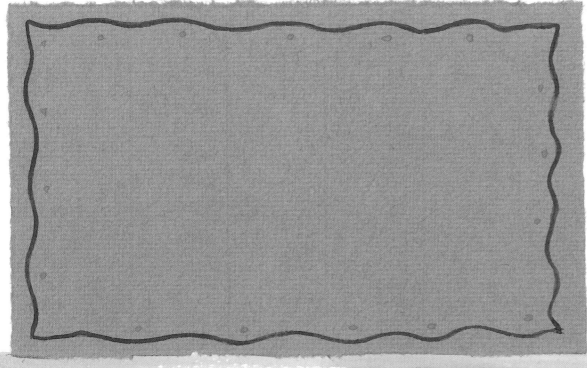

Date:
Place:

*Glue your first school
picture here.
If you remember the
names of your teacher
and friends, write them
down and use arrows to
show who in the
photograph is who!*

My Mom's Perfume

When you are older, one of your first memories will be of your mom's perfume. A mom smells delicious, a mom smells fresh, a mom smells like a mom! Here is a small square of paper to spray with her perfume.

my
mom's
perfume

Open the right side
of the transparent pocket.
Take out the paper inside and
spray it with your mom's perfume.
Put the paper back
into the pocket quickly.
Now, for a long time to come,
you will be able to enjoy this scent
you love so much.

My Mom by Heart

You believe you know your mom perfectly, like a house you've lived in for a very long time. And while it is true that you do know a thousand little things about her, sweet and secret things, there are also many things you may have forgotten to notice. For example, can you close your eyes and try to describe your mom's hands?
Let's try it…

Our Portraits
Do we look alike?

My mom

Me

Date: **Place:**

Date: **Place:**

Take a photo of your mom. Have her take a photo of you, too.
Then glue both photos above. Do you look alike?
If yes, use small arrows to indicate the similarities.

Mom, I find you very beautiful!

My mom with my eyes closed...

*Here are ten questions about your mom
that you must answer immediately, with your eyes closed.
Ask your mom to write down what you say!
If you get fewer than three right answers, then you must try again tomorrow with your family's help!*

What color are your mom's eyes?_____

What do her hands look like? _____

What does her voice sound like? Is it soft, gentle, high, or low? _____

What is the color of her hair? _____

And specifically today:

What does her hair look like? _____

Is she wearing makeup? If yes, what kind? _____
_____

Is she wearing glasses? If yes, what do they look like? _____
_____

What clothes is she wearing? _____
_____

And what do her shoes look like?_____

Is she wearing jewelry today? If yes, what does it look like? _____
_____

❤ Mom's Tastes

A mom has her tastes. We sense what they are when she buys us clothes we don't really like. Which of you knows the other's preferences best?

Blech!

My mom's tastes according to me

Her favorite color _____

Her favorite place _____

Her favorite object _____

Her favorite food _____

Her favorite outfit _____

Her favorite flower or tree _____

My tastes according to my mom

My favorite color _____

My favorite place _____

My favorite object _____

My favorite food _____

My favorite outfit _____

My favorite flower or tree _____

When both of you have answered these questions (on separate sheets of paper), copy the answers above and read the results together.

❤ My Mom's Bag of Secrets

Purse, backpack, tote bag, handbag, shoulder bag, or oversized wallet… Moms always bring a little of their house with them wherever they go. Usually we are not supposed to look inside. But let's imagine…

Draw all the things hidden in your mom's purse.

❤ My Mom's Moods

My mom is happy when
_____
_____

My mom gets angry when
_____
_____

My mom cannot be disturbed
when _____
_____

My mom laughs out loud when
_____
_____

Ha Ha Haaaaaa

My mom forgives me
when _____
_____
_____

What I must never ask my
mom is _____
_____
_____

What I can always ask my
mom is _____
_____
_____

Now me! I am in a very good
mood when _____
_____

Ha Haaa

*Tell me, Mom,
when you were little,
did your mom ever get angry at
you? If yes, why?*
_____
_____
_____

21

My Mom and Me
All the things she does...

A mom thinks and does a lot to make life happy. Some of her days are so full of responsibilities and details, they seem like giant puzzles. When that happens, putting together all the pieces is not an easy task!

While I am at school, she...

– buys food for the whole family

–

– works

–

–

–

Every morning, Mom...

– wakes me up

–

–

–

– hands me a snack

Fill in each piece of the puzzle.
Your brothers and sisters can help you,
and your dad can, too, of course!
Be sure to show the answers to your mom.
What does she think?

Between the time school is over and bedtime, Mom...

–

–

– helps me with my homework

–

– calls her best friend

– makes dinner

–

At bedtime, Mom…

– reminds me to brush my teeth!

–

–

–

–

– cuddles me

After school, Mom…

–

–

– is like a taxi service to soccer,
ballet, and all my other activities

–

–

– buys me clothes

–

–

When I am sick, Mom…

– finds someone to watch over me
if she can't

–

–

–

– brings me food on a tray

For my birthday, she…

– plans a party

– bakes me a special cake

–

– decorates our house

–

–

–

To make me happy, Mom…

– cooks macaroni and cheese

–

–

–

– repairs my favorite stuffed animal

–

–

On weekends or holidays, she…

–

–

– takes pictures of me with our family!

–

– reads a book she likes

–

Everything She Knows...

Most of the time, your mom knows what you like,
even if she sometimes makes mistakes. She knows
you and accepts everything about you, including
your weaknesses, though sometimes, those make
her frown. Your mom knows what you need. And
your mom also often guesses your secrets, the
beautiful ones as well as the awful ones!
And YOUR mom?

Ask your mom to write some of the things she knows about you in this window:
your likes, dislikes, strengths, weaknesses, dreams...

Everything We Haven't Told Each Other...

Even though you spend a lot of time with your mom,
you may not always share your thoughts and feelings
with each other. So, make a list here of how you see things.

Little list of how we see things

Mom's version

What I like doing with you: _____
_____
_____

What I dream of doing with you: _____
_____
_____

What I'd like not to do anymore with you:
_____
_____

What we do best together: _____
_____
_____

My version

What I like doing with you: _____
_____
_____

What I dream of doing with you: _____
_____
_____

What I'd like not to do anymore with you:
_____
_____

What we do best together: _____
_____
_____

Tell me, Mom, do you know which birthday present I liked best?
_____
_____

Tell me, Mom, which Mother's Day gift did you like best?
_____

Tell me, Mom, do you know which of my clothes I don't like?
_____
_____

Tell me, Mom, do you know what food I really don't like?
_____
_____

Learning About Life with Mom

As you grow older, you share with your mom, as well as your dad, more and more activities, hobbies, conversations, and laughs. These shared moments are like balloons floating up into the air.
One after another, they take off and fly…

Special moments with my mom

Here is a page to write about, draw, or glue photos of special moments you and your mom shared, such as a good laugh, a ski run, baking a cake…

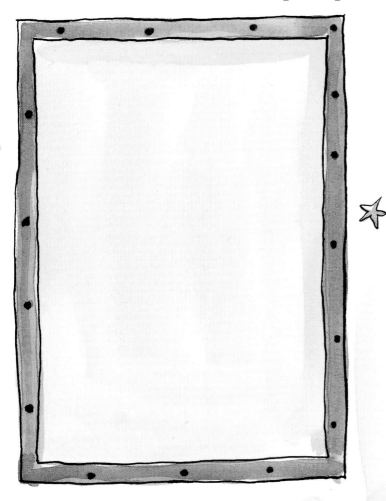

Date:
Place:

Date:
Place:

Date:
Place:

Date:
Place:

Your mom knows how to do many things very well.
Maybe she loves to garden, to cook, or to play the piano!
Ask her to write about the things she loves to do and why.

Things my mom loves to do!

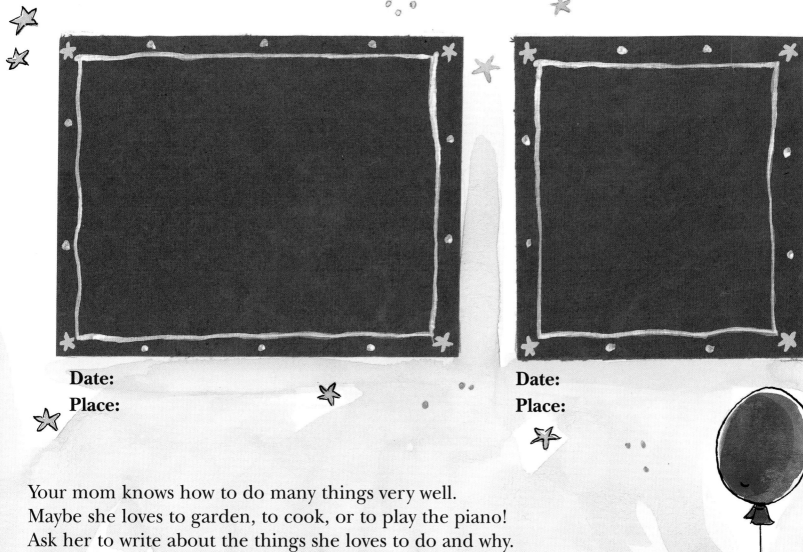

Thinking with Mom

A mom feeds and protects her children. She teaches them how to live and helps them to grow. She also guides them with her thoughts. How? By talking with them during meals, at bathtime, and even on the way to the store.

These little messages from your mom are like lanterns that brighten your path. Here is room to write down some of what your mom has taught you…

Answer me, Mom!

What are the three qualities in a person that are the most important to you? _____
_____
_____

What are parents for? Do we have to like them? _____
_____
_____

Do parents always like their children? And how do they love all of them at once? _____
_____
_____

Why do parents have secrets? _____
_____

And why do they sometimes fight? _____
_____
_____

Will I also be a dad or a mom one day? _____
_____

Is it difficult to be a mom?_____
_____
_____

Do you believe in God? Explain to me what you believe... _____
_____
_____
_____

Are you afraid of death? Do you believe there is life after death?_____
_____
_____

Why do we have to leave home one day?_____
_____
_____

When I'm a grown-up, what kinds of things will we do together? _____
_____
_____

If you become a grandmother, what would you like to be called?_____
_____

What do you wish for me the most in my grown-up life?_____
_____
_____
_____

My Mom and Her Life

A mom is not only a mom! She may also be a wife or companion, a friend, a daughter, or a sister.
Just like you, she has dreams, ideas, and interests all her own…
In fact, some moms have so many projects and responsibilities, you will sometimes hear them exclaim:
"Right now, I'm juggling!"
(This means that they may be a little overwhelmed but are probably still okay…)
Can you list some of your mom's projects and interests?

In the juggling balls above, write or draw the names of your mom's best friends and some of the things that they like to do together.

My Mom and Her Work

A lot of moms have jobs outside of what they take care of at home. On the subject of working, children often have an opinion.

Some say:

"It's good because she earns money!"

Others declare:

"It's not great because we don't get to see her enough!"

And you, what do you think? Before telling your mom, ask her to clearly explain to you what she does, and what she likes or doesn't like about her job.

Tell me, Mom, when you were my age, did you know what you wanted to be when you grew up?

_____

_____

Tell me, Mom, do you like your job? Or would you prefer to do another job? If you would, which one?

_____

_____

Tell me, Mom, which part of your job do you like most? Which part are you best at? And why?

_____

_____

Tell me, Mom, did you go to school to be able to do your job? If yes, what did you study?

_____

My mom's job

_____

_____

_____

_____

_____

_____

_____

_____

_____

_____

_____

_____

From Mom to Mom

The moms of the past were different from the moms of today. Their jobs, their lives at home, their place in society, their clothes, their hairdos, their makeup, their hobbies, their tastes…many things were not the same. And yet, if we could ask their children, "Why do you love your mom?" their answers would be very close to the answers of today's children.

So, from mom to mom, and with the passing of time, a continuous thread unwinds. It shows all the good reasons children love their moms so much!

She is warm.

She protects me.

She is gentle.

She listens to me.

She is sweet.

She gave birth to me.

She is very beautiful.

She loves me.

She loves to cuddle with me.

She makes me good things to eat.

She shows me how to take care of the garden.

She hangs my pictures on the wall.

She takes care of me.

She understands me.

She loves to read with me.

She helps me.

She keeps my secrets.

She listens to me.

She helps me to grow up.

She explains things to me.

She is happy when I come home from school.

She is brave.

She is patient almost all of the time.

She knows what I need.

My Mom and Her Family

A mom is also the daughter of a mom and a dad and the granddaughter of four grandparents, just like you!

Ask your mom to tell you more about her parents (your maternal grandparent. What are their names? When were they born? Where did they grow up? What were their jobs? What did they like to do? What about her grandparents (your great-grandparents)? Then fill in the spaces in the little house on the next page. Don't forget to include your mom's brothers and sisters (your uncles and aunts), if she has them!

Once the information in the house is complete, you'll know a lot more about your mom's family, and so a lot more about your own family, too!

Glue photos of each of your maternal grandparents below.
Does your mom look like either one of them? Do you?

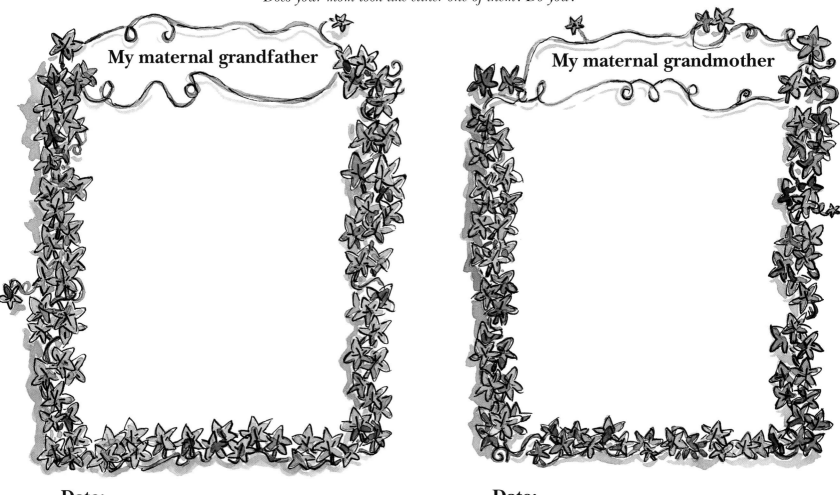

My maternal grandfather

My maternal grandmother

Date:

Place:

Date:

Place:

In each of the little windows, fill in the names and birthdays of each member of your mom's family.

My mom

My uncles and aunts
(Mom's brothers and sisters)

My maternal
grandfather
(Mom's dad)

My maternal
grandmother
(Mom's mom)

My maternal great-grandparents
(Mom's grandparents)

Tell me, Mom, what else do you know about our family?

Where did our family originate? Where does our name come from? Are there any famous people in our family?

_____

_____

_____

_____

My Mom As a Baby

Not long ago, your mom was a baby, too! It's hard to believe that she is the one you see in the photos, nestled in the arms of her own mom or perhaps trying to learn to walk!

Yet, it wasn't so long ago…

Do you know when and where your mom was born?
Do you know the story of her birth?
Ask her to tell you, or better yet, suggest to one of your maternal grandparents (your mom's mom or dad) to write down what he or she remembers.

Tell me, Mom, did your parents organize a religious ceremony after your birth? If yes, what kind was it?
_____
_____
_____

The story of my mom's birth

My mom's godfather and godmother
_____
_____
_____

_____
_____
_____
_____
_____
_____
_____
_____
_____
_____
_____
_____

Tell me, Mom, how old was your mom when you were born?

_____

Tell me, Mom, what kind of baby were you? (big eater, sleepy, excited, fussy...)

_____
_____

Tell me, Mom, what are your first and middle names? And were you named after anyone in particular?

_____
_____
_____

Tell me, Mom, who took care of you when you were a baby?

_____
_____
_____

Tell me, Mom, what is your astrogical sign?

_____
_____

Photo of my mom as a baby

Look at this photo closely with your mom and show, with arrows, all the details that have changed. Does anything look different now from how it did when your mom was a baby?

Date:

Place:

My Mom As a Little Girl

To experience life, to learn, to play, to dream, to be afraid, to sulk, to be sick, to play dress-up, to love, to fight, to do naughty things, to be punished and forgiven…and then to do it all over again! Yes, your mom has gone through these things, too.

Since she was a little girl, a lot of things have changed in the lives of children. Here are four pages devoted to discovering who your mom was when she was your age.

My favorite photo(s) of my mom as a little girl

Glue one or two photos of your mom as a girl, at different ages if possible, with her family, her friends, her toys…
And don't forget to include the dates!

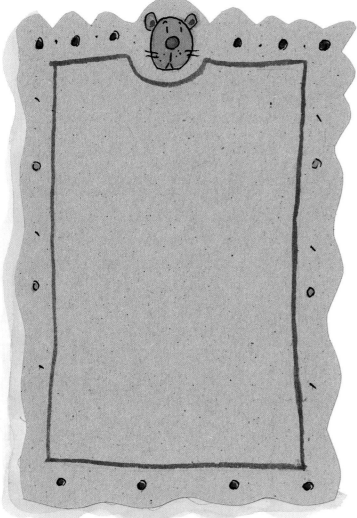

Date:　　　**Place:**

Date:　　　**Place:**

A day in the life of my mom when she was a little girl...

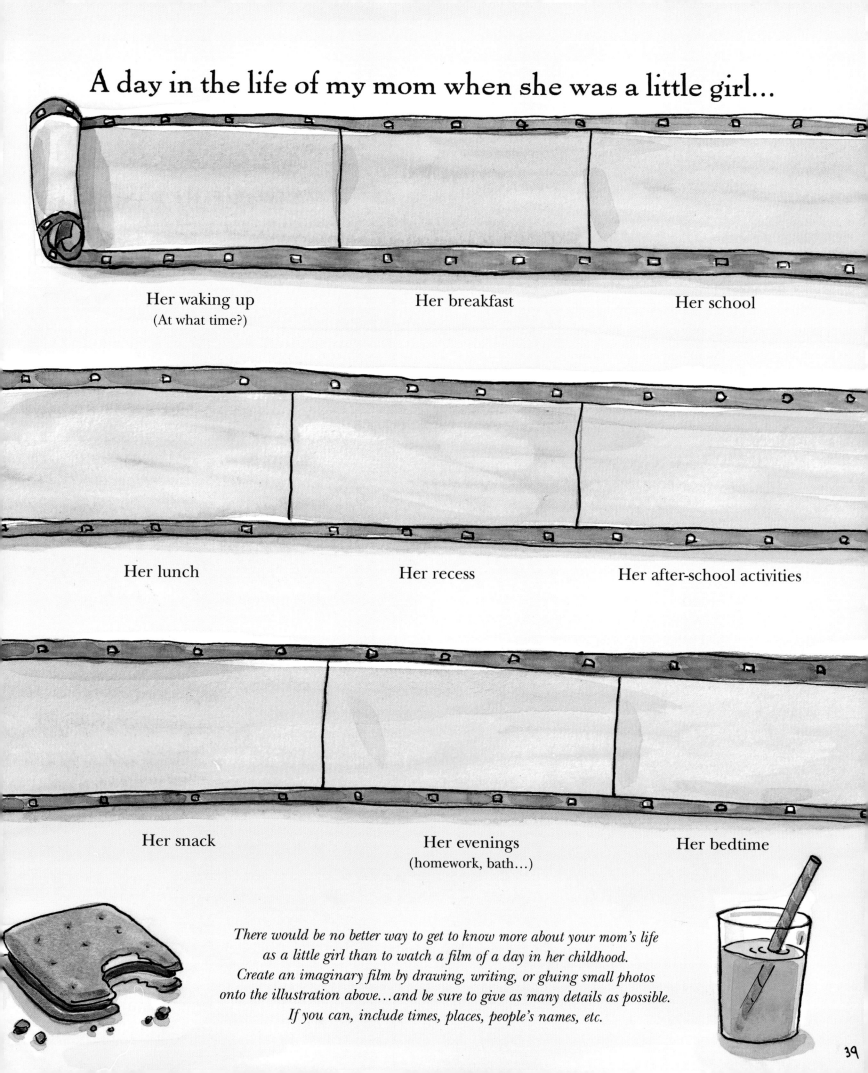

Her waking up
(At what time?)

Her breakfast

Her school

Her lunch

Her recess

Her after-school activities

Her snack

Her evenings
(homework, bath...)

Her bedtime

There would be no better way to get to know more about your mom's life as a little girl than to watch a film of a day in her childhood. Create an imaginary film by drawing, writing, or gluing small photos onto the illustration above...and be sure to give as many details as possible. If you can, include times, places, people's names, etc.

39

Tell me, Mom!

Your family life

What did your parents like to call you? _____
_____

Were they strict or easygoing? Do you remember
what things were against the rules? _____
_____
_____

If you had brothers and sisters, what things did
you do with them? _____
_____

And with your cousins? _____
_____

Did you help out at home? Did you have chores?
_____

Did you get to see your grandparents often?
What did you call them? _____
_____

Where did they live? _____
How did your family celebrate your birthday? Did
you have a birthday cake and a party? _____
_____

And how did you celebrate the holidays? _____
_____
_____

Tell me, Mom, was your family religious? If yes, which religion(s) did they practice? _____ _____

Your life and its secrets

Where did you live? _____
_____

What did your bedroom look like? _____
_____
_____
_____

Did you have a favorite toy? _____
_____

How did you like to dress? _____
_____

What did you love to eat? _____
_____

And what did you hate to eat? _____
_____

Did you ever have temper tantrums? _____
_____

Did you ever get sick? _____
_____

What is your most beautiful childhood memory?
_____
_____
_____

And your worst one? _____
_____
_____

Tell me, Mom, were you ever allowed to try out your mom's makeup?

_____
_____
_____

Tell me, Mom, who in your family did you get along with best? And why?

_____
_____
_____

Tell me, Mom, what was the naughtiest thing you ever did?

_____
_____
_____

Tell me, Mom, did you have a boyfriend?

_____
_____

Tell me, Mom, did you get an allowance each week? If yes, how much?

_____
_____

Your life with others and at school

Did you have a best friend?_____

_____

What were your favorite school subjects and activities?_____

_____

What kind of school did you attend?_____

_____

_____

Did you eat in the cafeteria? What did you usually have for lunch?_____

_____

_____

What kind of student were you?_____

_____

Was there a subject you were extra good at?

_____

_____

Did you do your homework by yourself?_____

_____

Did you like school? If yes or if no, why?

_____

_____

_____

Did you walk or take the bus to school?_____

_____

Where did you spend your vacations and with whom?_____

_____

My Mom As a Teenager

When she was 13 years old, your mom became a teenager. She went to her first dance, maybe started wearing lipstick, and perhaps kissed her first boyfriend! And let's not forget, maybe she got her first pimple, too…but shh! She is the only one who can tell you about that…

Photo of my mom as a teenager!

Date: **Place:**

My Mom As a Young Woman

She's 20…22…25 years old, and your mom has now become a young woman. For some moms, this was not long ago. For other moms, it was quite some time ago. But for all moms, it was an important time, the time when they stepped into adult life. What was your mom like as a young woman? Was she athletic? Did she have a job? Was she in love? Did she travel? Was she already a mom? What did she dream her future would be like?

Ask your mom to write below about the young woman she was.
Then, ask someone who knew her then (perhaps your dad or your grandparents) to tell you their memories of her at 20.
Copy this statement next to your mom's. Is it different?

My mom at 20

Through her eyes!

Through the eyes of _____

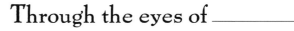

Meeting My Dad

To have a child, there must first be a mom and a dad who met… But it is rare that a child knows exactly how, where, and when his mom and dad first met. And who fell in love first?

It is interesting to know the happy turn of events that brought us here!

Ask each of your parents to write down on a small sheet of paper how they met (where, when?). Glue both versions below, and compare them, of course!

Mom's version

Dad's version

Date:

Place:

Ask your mom to give you a photo of the time when she and your dad were newly in love or at their wedding. If your mom chooses a picture of the wedding, ask her to tell you the story of this big day…

Our Family

House mom, sun mom, fruit mom, life mom. A mom definitely has a big heart—big enough to shelter all her children and the rest of the family, too… So, we need to share our moms, and sometimes we'd like to forget that!

Date: **Place:**

Glue a photo above of your family with as many people as possible.
If possible, include everybody's name and age!

Those Eyes...

One of the most wonderful things about your mom is that, even when you're grown up, she will still be your mom! No matter where you are in the world or what you do, you will always be a part of her heart and mind.

And if you feel lost or confused from time to time, you can always remember her eyes and be filled with all the love she has for you!

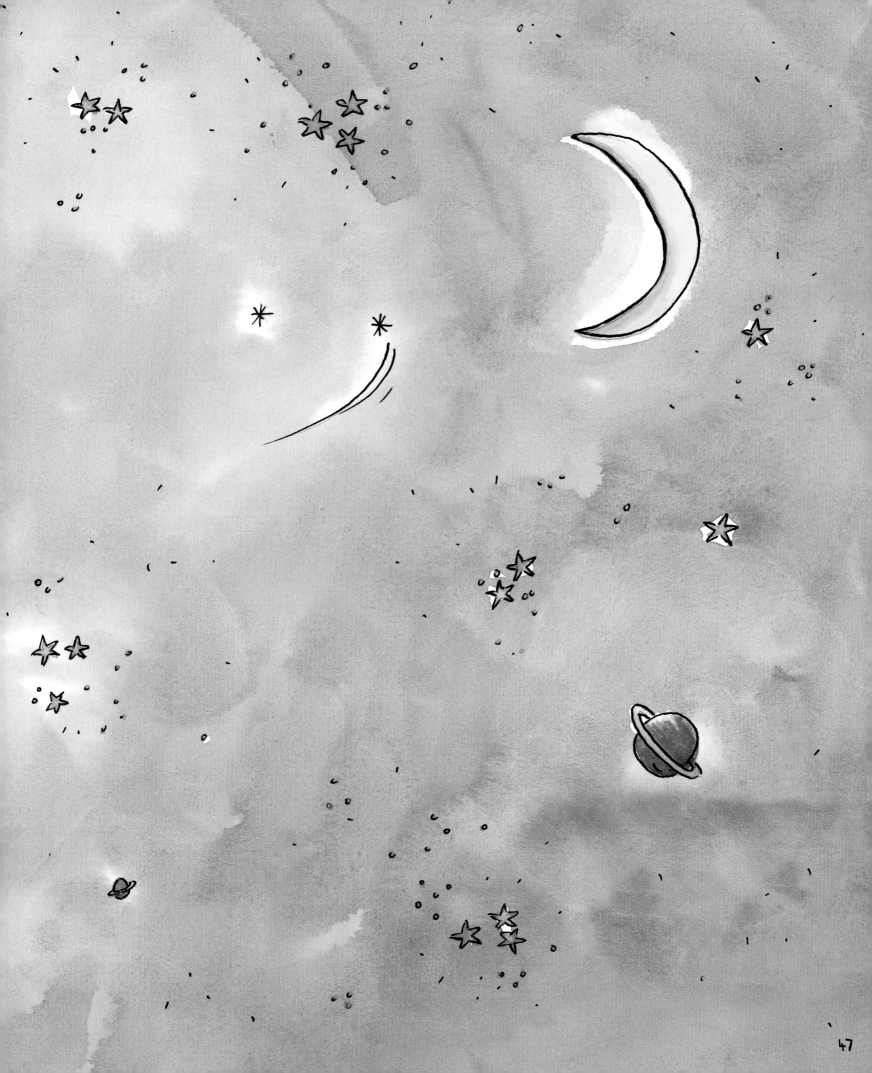

Contents

Like a House... 4

Life Before You Were Born 6

My Birth 9

My Firsts 12

My Life As a Toddler .14

My Mom's Perfume 16

My Mom by Heart 18

My Mom and Me 22

Learning About Life with Mom 26

Thinking with Mom 28

My Mom and Her Life 30

My Mom and Her Work 31

From Mom to Mom 32

My Mom and Her Family 34

My Mom As a Baby 36

My Mom As a Little Girl 38

My Mom As a Teenager 42

My Mom As a Young Woman 43

Meeting My Dad 44

Our Family 45

Those Eyes... 46

The details in this book were recorded by

_____ and _____

at _____

Cataloging-in-Publication Data has
been applied for.
ISBN 0-8109-4820-6

Illustrations and original text copyright © 2003
Diane Barbara and Christine Donnier
English translation copyright © 2004
Harry N. Abrams, Inc.

Published in 2004 by Harry N. Abrams,
Incorporated, New York
All rights reserved. No part of the contents
of this book may be reproduced without the
written permission of the publisher.

Printed and bound in Belgium
10 9 8 7 6 5 4 3 2 1

Harry N. Abrams, Inc.
100 Fifth Avenue
New York, NY 10011
www.abramsbooks.com

Abrams is a subsidiary of
LA MARTINIÈRE
GROUPE